WITHDRAWN

Guess Who
Changes

Adivina quién
cambia

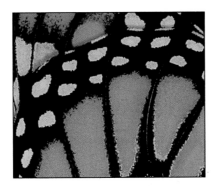

Sharon Gordon

Marshall Cavendish
Benchmark
New York

Here I am!

My mother left me on this leaf.

———◆———

¡Aquí estoy!

Mi madre me dejó en esta hoja.

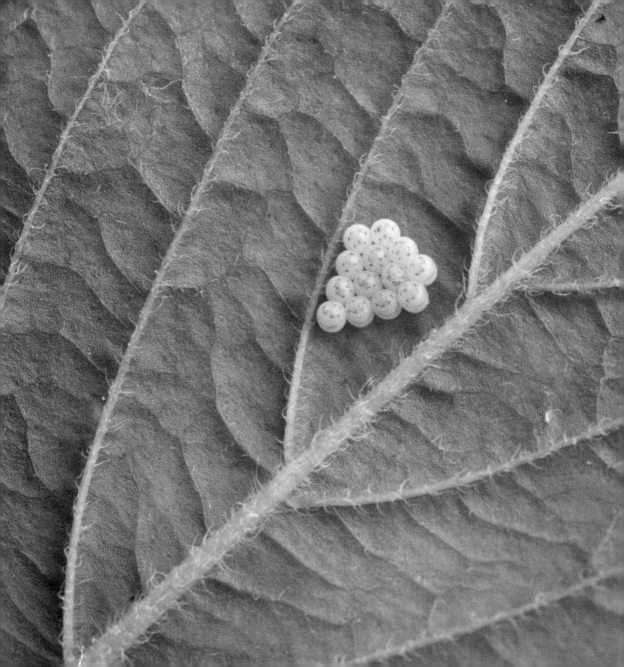

I am inside this tiny egg.

I am ready to hatch.

❖

Estoy dentro de este huevo diminuto.

Estoy lista para romper la cáscara.

The egg pops open.

I crawl out.

———————❖———————

El huevo se abre y salgo arrastrándome.

It is easy with 16 legs.

I have become a caterpillar.

Es fácil hacerlo con 16 patas.

Ahora soy una oruga.

I am so hungry!

I eat and eat and eat.

❖

¡Tengo tanta hambre!

Como y como y como.

Now I do not fit in my old skin.

It splits open.

A new skin is inside.

———❖———

Ahora no quepo en mi piel anterior.

Se parte y hay una nueva piel dentro.

I keep eating and growing.

My old skin falls off each time.

Sigo comiendo y creciendo.

Mi piel anterior se cae una y otra vez.

One day, I crawl under a leaf.

I shed my skin for the last time.

Un día me arrastro debajo de una hoja.

Me quito la piel por última vez.

A hard shell grows around me.

Now I am a *pupa*.

———◆———

Una capa dura crece a mi alrededor.

Ahora soy una *crisálida*.

Inside, I am changing.

I am growing four wings.

———◆———

Dentro, estoy cambiando.

Me están creciendo cuatro alas.

My hard shell splits open.
See how I have changed!

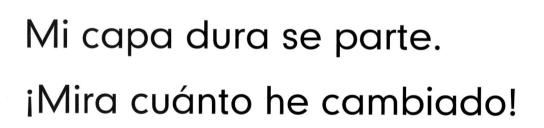

Mi capa dura se parte.
¡Mira cuánto he cambiado!

I stretch my colorful wings.

I am ready to fly.

Who am I?

❖

Extiendo mis alas de colores.

Estoy lista para volar.

¿Quién soy?

I am a butterfly!

¡Soy una mariposa!

Who am I?

¿Quién soy?

caterpillar
oruga

egg
huevo

pupa
crisálida

28

skin
piel

wings
alas

Challenge Word

pupa A caterpillar that has grown a hard shell on the outside.

Palabra avanzada

crisálida Una oruga que se cubre de una capa dura por fuera.

Index

Índice

About the Author
Datos biográficos de la autora

Sharon Gordon has written many books for young children. She has always worked as an editor. Sharon and her husband Bruce have three children, Douglas, Katie, and Laura, and one spoiled pooch, Samantha. They live in Midland Park, New Jersey.

❖

Sharon Gordon ha escrito muchos libros para niños. Siempre ha trabajado como editora. Sharon y su esposo Bruce tienen tres niños, Douglas, Katie y Laura, y una perra consentida, Samantha. Viven en Midland Park, Nueva Jersey.

31

With thanks to Nanci Vargus, Ed.D. and
Beth Walker Gambro, reading consultants

Marshall Cavendish Benchmark
99 White Plains Road
Tarrytown, New York 10591-9001
www.marshallcavendish.us

Library of Congress Cataloging-in-Publication Data

Gordon, Sharon.
[Guess who changes. Spanish & English]
Guess who changes = Adivina quién cambia / Sharon Gordon. — Bilingual ed.
p. cm. — (Bookworms. Guess who? = Adivina quién)
Includes index.
ISBN-13: 978-0-7614-2461-1 (bilingual edition)
ISBN-10: 0-7614-2461-X (bilingual edition)
ISBN-13: 978-0-7614-2380-5 (Spanish edition)
ISBN-10: 0-7614-1558-0 (English edition)
1. Butterflies—Juvenile literature. I. Title. II. Title: Adivina quién cambia. III. Series: Gordon, Sharon. Bookworms.
Guess who? (Spanish & English)

QL544.2.G6718 2006b
595.78'9—dc22
2006016812

Spanish Translation and Text Composition by Victory Productions, Inc.
www.victoryprd.com

Photo Research by Anne Burns Images

Cover Photo by: *Visuals Unlimited*/Rick & Nora Bowers

The photographs in this book are used with permission and through the courtesy of: *Visuals Unlimited*:
pp. 1, 25, 29 (right) Rick and Nora Bowers; pp. 7, 17, 29 (left) Dick Poe; pp. 9, 28 (upper left) Wally Eberhart;
p. 11 Bill Beatty; p. 15 John Gerlock; pp. 19, 27, 28 (bottom) Bob Wilson; p. 21 Gary Meszaros; p. 23 D. Cavagnaro.
Corbis: p. 3 Jim Sugar Photography; pp. 5, 28 (upper right) George Lepp. *Animals, Animals*: p. 13 Patti Murray.

Series design by Becky Terhune

Printed in Malaysia
1 3 5 6 4 2